HOW TO DROWN A BOY

J. BRUCE FULLER

LOUISIANA STATE UNIVERSITY PRESS

BATON ROUGE

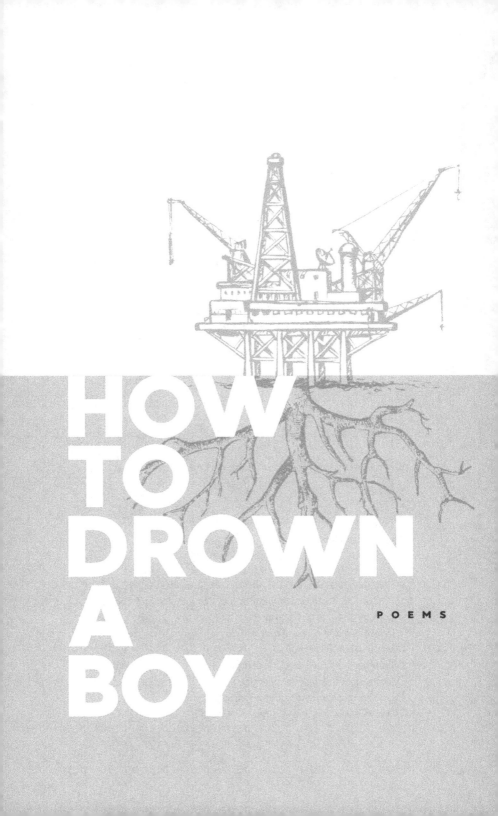

HOW
TO
DROWN
A
BOY

POEMS

Published by Louisiana State University Press
lsupress.org

LSU Press Paperback Original

Designer: Michelle A. Neustrom
Typeface: Whitman, text; Metropolis, display

Cover illustration: *Oil Roots*, 2022, by Bradley Alan Ivey

Library of Congress Cataloging-in-Publication Data
Names: Fuller, J. Bruce, author.
Title: How to drown a boy : poems / J. Bruce Fuller.
Other titles: How to drown a boy (Compilation)
Description: Baton Rouge : Louisiana State University Press, 2024.
Identifiers: LCCN 2023024708 (print) | LCCN 2023024709 (ebook) |
    ISBN 978-0-8071-8128-7 (paperback) | ISBN 978-0-8071-8144-7 (pdf) |
    ISBN 978-0-8071-8143-0 (epub)
Subjects: LCGFT: Poetry.
Classification: LCC PS3606.U543 H69 2024 (print) | LCC PS3606.U543
    (ebook) | DDC 811/.6—dc23/eng/20230920
LC record available at https://lccn.loc.gov/2023024708
LC ebook record available at https://lccn.loc.gov/2023024709

Mon fils,
ç'est pour toi

Papa,
je comprends

CONTENT

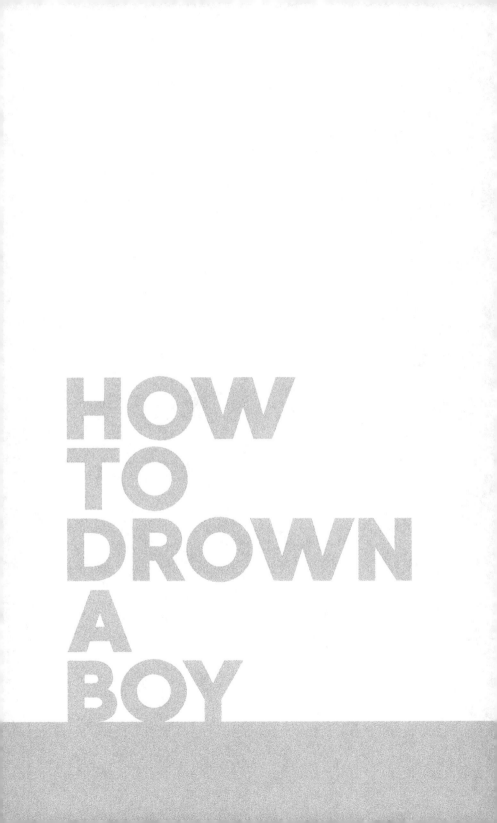

HOW
TO
DROWN
A
BOY

How to Drown a Boy

Not with water, but with sweat,
you work the boy until he cries.

At the barn faucet, think of your own father,
cup your hands and tell the boy
to look deep inside this well,
make him drink from your hands,
make him drink until he swells, make
him taste the salt and split nails,
cracked knuckles, bone, and blood.

Tell him this blood is the life I have given,
this blood the covenant, that you must always
measure your life against mine.

Now sneak him the whiskey
behind the shed where his mother can't see,
show him that this is what a man has earned,
and just a taste because he's only a boy,
with too much of his mother in him.
A sip more and he will learn.

And if the sharpness of the still
leaves him weak,
or the swing of the hammer
wears him out,
and if he squirms
at the trigger pull
to give the doe a chance to flee,
then walk the boy down to the river
and baptize him there
with your own two hands.

~ ~ ~

The Gift at Diridon Station

And I met a man once at Diridon Station
who asked me for a cigarette and I seen
he was a traveler and I seen he had been lost.
And I give him one but won't let him pay.
He offers twice but I won't let him pay.
And I heard in his voice the voice of home
and I seen in his face the face of my father.

So I asked him where he was from
and he said a long ways off a thousand miles east
and I said me too and I said whereabouts
and he said Kentucky and I said Louisiana
and we smoked together and talked ourselves
back home for a while.

And he told me what he seen of the world.
And he told me he ain't seen much
of what it says in the Good Book.
And I told him I met good people
who ain't never even heard of Jesus.
And I told him I met a woman who prayed
kneeling on grains of rice for hours
until she couldn't walk and her husband
come home and beat her for not having
supper ready. We all His children they say.

And they say Jesus did miracles at Cana
in Galilee but I was taught to fear the wine
and reminded with a heavy hand.
And they say when you have a houseguest
treat him like family cause he might be Jesus

come to test us. And I think about Jesus
knocking on that door asking.

As I left I wished him luck on his journey
and as I was walking off he called to me.
Him pulling around in his pack for payment
and me knowing better than to refuse him again.
And he pulls out a double-bladed Barlow knife
bent and mangled and stainless steel
and been lord-knows-where. And he holds
it out in his hand like a sacrament
and I take it from his hand like it's the Lord's
own flesh. I say it's too much and he might need it
and he says naw I got a hundred of em
and I know he don't
but we both know this ritual and anyways
a man can't be beholden to another man
like it says in the Book.

Remembering My Father Who Went Off to Work

I think of my father, gone
for months, and the places
he went for work,
and, though he said nothing much
upon returning, the wonders
our mother would tell us
about the places he went,
and realize that there wasn't
much to tell of his trips,
each place much the same
to a pipefitter, building
Wal-Marts in small towns
the same as ours, pipelines
that looked the same except
for maybe a difference
in temperature or elevation,
but sometimes, how he would
describe a bird we'd never seen,
or snow, as strange to us
as the moon, or sometimes,
that far-off look he'd get,
what I now understand to mean.

I know now what you left there, Papa,
tobacco spit on churned earth,
right-of-ways that stretch
as far as a man's mind can stand,
until it breaks, and you heave
out your guts full of beer
in an abandoned mall parking lot,

working shutdowns until every
refinery looks the same
and you lose your way
in the crawlspaces that stretch
beneath entire rivers,
the way mountains make you feel
small at first then even less
until you pray for a flat,
clear horizon to show you
the way home, the faces
of your sons you've forgotten
a thousand times in a bar
in Topeka, or Amarillo, or Jackson,
so when the local girl
with a thing for roughnecks
sidles up, you see in her face
the faces you miss and you reach
out for the life you left behind.

Poem with an Image of My Brother

I see it often, a flash
across my mind before sleep,
or sometimes, while making love,
or once, when my car swerved
and my mind thought I was done
so it showed me his dusty knees
one last time, before the end.
My brother playing in the dirt
on his hands and knees, old dog
collar around his skinny neck,
and a chain stretching up
to a line strung between two trees
that allowed the dogs to run
back and forth along a dirt path,
and I am just out of frame,
spindly legged and watching,
always watching.

St. John the Baptist

Shirtless and sweating in the summer,
I inoculate sheep. They will not still
as I straddle and hold them with my knees,
aim the needle at their jugular veins.
Too deep and the needle will pierce
clean through.
                    Are these the lambs
you shepherded through the wilderness
to wash and give that final protection,
their blood so precious as to require
a vaccine of pure spirit?
                    I wash
the woolen filth from my arms
and chest, bend down and place
my neck beneath the barn faucet,
bend down
            humbly.

Parable

When I am low and thinking darkly
there often comes to mind a moment
from my childhood of two brothers
about our own age named Cain and Abel
not the boys from the Book
but the sons of a friend of my father
who invited us to stay one Christmas
when we were down on our luck again
and how after we played all afternoon
in the yard with an old foam football
and ate together boiled shrimp with rice
we sat down to watch the boys open their presents
and I didn't realize until Abel
opened his to find the same football
two chunks of foam torn by the dogs
how none of the toys were in packages
and many I had seen earlier in their room
and how I couldn't keep the shame
from my face as I met Cain's eyes
and his look was a stone I have carried with me
on some days as heavy as the way
he placed his hand on his brother's shoulder
and O God how I can't find the lesson
in all of this O dear God of terrible mercies

Cochon du Lait

1.

The first of September,
two chickens hung
on a nail, necks
wrung, she salts
the water to boil.

In the crisp air
outside the camper
kitchen, her boys
chop and cord
firewood.

She watches them
while she works,
the sound
of wood breaking,
wings snapped
from the body.
The labor of it all.

2.

Their father prepares
the pit. Shirtless,
he digs postholes
for the tin shed
he has built
to cover the pig.

Light reflected
off the dark water
of Woolen Lake,
scent of cypress trees
turned brown
from bagworms.

Nearby,
a blue heron
waits for a flash
of silver.

Nothing wasted here.
He digs without
bitterness or self-
pity. His boys
pile the wood.

3.

A boy hidden deep
in the brush waits
at clearing's edge.

At dusk a sow
comes with two
piglets rooting
in the half-light.

To hunt the hog
is to feel what
the hog feels
in the thicket bramble.

The boy edges
forward, but father
stays his hand.
This is not an act
of kindness. They wait
for the boar.

4.

The boar sleeps
in his clay bed.
What dreams
for those reared
in heat?

The father wakes
his sons in the night,
hands them shovels
to turn the coals.

For three nights
he teaches
them this.

5.

Early September,
a bacchanal.
Bonfires across
the yard burn
the cypress wood,
bagworms and all.

Cousins arrive,
then men with beards
and reddened lips.
Then musicians
with guitars,
banjos, accordions.
O catin, they cry,
Donnez-moi
mon chapeau.

Parents become children,
and children run
wild all night.

6.

Morning comes.

Across the lake
the water stills,
and owl calls carry far.

The fire has gone low,
and the pit
must be filled again,
but today we will make
no work.

People scattered
across furniture,
children on the floor
in sleeping bags.

The sun lights the room.
I refuse to wake.

they said

they said beau was on that crystal and that's why he lost so much
   weight
come back from summer break looking long and thin
so the coaches moved him from left tackle to outside linebacker

and i was so skinny that kids made jokes and threw food at me in
   the cafeteria
they said eat a cheeseburger you couillon they said

and i didn't want to be skinny no more and i didn't want to be
   weak no more
and i didn't want to do crystal even though beau was popular now
even though his new girlfriend was a real dixie queen
and when the ark-la-miss news said he was dead
i didn't understand and i didn't know they also called it meth

~~~

Float the Bones

It begins, as it must,
with those of us who live
on the slip of fringe
where water meets bladed grass.
It raises up the root and bramble,
bone and bark, and stirs them in the heat.
If only a heart could swell
as much as this gospel.
The water pushes up the caskets of the poor.
Three days of rain and we rise
from beneath stone slabs,
for what ground could hold us
if Jesus wept?
Our wild hair swirls
and we forget our bodies.
Bring out the boats
to salvage both living and dead.
Bury the wolves
until our bones float and mingle
and turn to ground again.

In the Backwater

The water rises slowly—a creeping drown
measured on cattail stalks

It consumes the banks
scuttling the pelicans from their feast
in our fishnet pens

We count the cinderblocks
weigh our options in inches
consult our almanacs
and revive our rituals

We dance quietly on plywood floors
and shake salt at the water beneath the door

Madonna of the Serpent

Maman was not pleased
when she heard how we lured
the snakes out of the water
with our crawfish nets
and tramped down on their heads
with our black rubber boots.
The moccasins were as gray
as the wet sky. We were not bitten.
Let 'em alone, Papa told her,
a boy ought not fear a snake,
but she did fear, and she marched
us firmly out of our wet clothes
and into the house.
A mother knows much of good
and evil, but she never knew the feel
of the snake's dark body,
the crunch of its skull underfoot,
nor how her foot
helped to guide my own.

The Gar

A quick strike, near miss,
too sharp for a white perch,
and of those we pulled in
so many of them scarred
around their tails, red
lesions around the back fins,
so when I asked Papa why we killed
the gar he said because they eat
the sac-a-lait in our fishing holes
which you know already,
and he was too busy pulling in
the long prehistoric body of a gar
to understand my question, so all afternoon
I brought the boat paddle down hard
on rows of sharp teeth,
until dusk, as we banked the boat,
he said again, *because*
they eat what we eat.

Alluvial

I am thinking of lessons
my father never taught me,
and those he did.

There is danger on every corner,
rivers of asphalt waiting
to claim limbs. So too
in the darkened water,
an ancient animal waiting below,
the stillness at bank's edge.

What I remember is this:
Bubbles from the bottom, boy,
step back.

Sit Still

I watch for deer
through the kitchen window,
for any rustle at woods' edge,
as we did when we were young.

Small boys take small steps
and the wood grows darker
each year.

Deeper in, a canal
cuts through, the trees
beyond, unfamiliar.
In summer, when the canal
water is low, fish writhe
in filmy pools, a feast for egrets
and boys with rakes.

A month into flood season,
the water is no longer hidden
in the earth, and the horses
have come in from the rain.

The water has reached
the woods' edge, and the deer
have come out, ears twitching,
nervous. Sit still.
They smell the horses,
the boat motors, the oil in the water,
and step back beyond the trees.

they said

they said the lord wasn't gonna flood the world no more
but he must have forgot about us so we took what we could
from the waterlogged houses mostly guns mostly pill bottles
mostly things we could sell no questions asked

in my neighbor's house i smashed the door of a gun cabinet
and the deer etched on the glass scattered

they said take that shit hurry the fuck up
but i just stood there looking til we left
they said you a pussy you coulda made a fortune

they said édouard got sent to angola
and come back with a swastika on his neck

~~~

The Dissenter's Ground

Dip him in the river who loves water.
   ~ ~ ~
Expect poison from the standing water.

    —William Blake, *The Marriage of Heaven and Hell*

1.

    Bunhill Fields, London

William,
Would I ask you this if I knew you?
Would you answer,
or would the angels fall silent and fail
to speak, their words muffled and lost
through time and ether
and unconsecrated earth?

It's just that I have no one else to turn to.

2.

Cameron Parish, Louisiana

Here is what I know:
When the sun sets on Rutherford Beach
and the wind off the gulf lifts brown water
over shelled sands, the oil rigs
on the horizon no longer remind me of God.

3.

They say in fifty years
the sea level will rise
all the way to Natchez.
This is prophecy of my age,
that this soupy ground
will be seabed again.

4.

William,
We live on borrowed land,
delta mud laid thick
by flood after flood,
the warbling, shifting muck
of home.

It shapes you, this instability,
this accretion of silt and image.
This is our homily as the waters rise
around us, that we revel
in the uncertainty of the seasons,
that we praise this tradition
of inevitable transience.

We will take drowning too far.

5.

What crawling villain preaches abstinence
& wraps himself in fat of lambs?
—*America: A Prophecy*

Urizen is sleeping, William,
and what has formed in that darkness
is this:

Oil, that prophecy
of your Industrial Revolution,
come to shackle us.

As a child I thought the rigs
were gods, and the men
who went to work them
had gone on to Heaven.

6.

Louisiane

The God of the Flood
still lives here.

You can see his practiced hand
among the dead cypress stobs
that dot the living water.

My father explained to me
how water overcomes land,
how one turn of the river
can make a field or forest
into a museum of skeleton trees,
but when I asked *why*
he said nothing.

Around here, we don't pray for rain.

7.

I too am a born dissenter.

There is a deep belief that lives
in the water and the fields,
in a way of life that has endured
for generations, forged in heat
and work, and the fear
of a vengeful God.

Where is that belief in my heart?

When I look my father in the face
I am ashamed.

8.

Albion

In the catacombs of St. Paul's
I found your marbled face, William,
but the stone was silent, the prophecy blunted.
Your bronze bust in the Poet's Corner
spoke no answers.
But these are not the trappings
of a living prophet.
I imagined you then, receiving visions,
naked in your garden at Felpham.

I have asked my questions to the void,
to the gods, to the earth,
to the muses, to a man
buried quietly in the Dissenter's Ground,
Bunhill Fields, London.
Farther and farther this doubt echoes,
and I am Adam in the garden, palms open.

Levee Patrol

Nights like these are made for trouble.
When the river is high
you've got to watch what you're doing.
A log can boil up from the bottom,
knock a man right out of the boat.
The currents don't act right,
like an animal that smells a coyote,
unpredictable.
They say there are men
from the Mississippi side
that want to blow a hole
in our levee. Six generations
since your grandfather
hacked a farm from these
pine forests, and I'll be damned
if somebody's gonna wash it away now.
Keep your finger on that trigger
and watch for a spark.
Down there in the bottoms
the fog gathers together
like the congregation of a church
we aren't allowed to join.
Son, there are some things
we can never be a part of.

The Men on the Levee

Of the men on the levee,
I will say this:
they were brave and terrible,
their eyes wild as the river.

I will also say this:
such men of power
and wild eyes like the river
cannot sleep easy in its shadow.

Such men of power
fear what the water will take,
will not sleep easy in its shadow,
knowing what stands before its swell.

Fearing what the river will take,
the poor men of the basin
knew what stood before the water's swell,
raised their hands to the sky.

The poor men of the delta
went to fight the river as well,
raising their hands to the sky,
singing, *What water will come, will come.*

They went to fight the river
those brave and terrible men
singing *What water will come, will come,*
What water will come, will come.

Charaxos

I would not be so hard on you, brother,
as that great mistress once was with Charaxos.

When you go to sea, to the oil rigs,
let me remember the peril and judge not

your mistakes on the shore.
It is not my place.

My place is to remember you, curly blond,
among the turnrows hunting doves—

of all our brothers, the best shot by far—
let me remember the tracker in you,

the hunt forever stirring in you.
And let me remember too

all the unrest that lives in me.
We are the same. Like our father

the same. We wrestle, with the sea,
with a power too great for us.

they said

they said blood is made in the bones but oil comes from the gulf
and when the storms rock the rigs the chaplain takes confessions
and the boys cross themselves all night

they said big dan got blown up and burned all over
and now he lights his cigarettes with his ring finger
they said the settlement money is long gone

they said when the rigs catch fire some boys jump
they said them boys burn and even the water can't put em out

~ ~ ~

Boy, Age 9

Hunting squirrels with my father,
I learned to track them through the trees,
to walk beneath their rustle and chase.
When the squirrels noticed us they froze
and lay flat against the mottled bark.
It was my job he said to walk noticeably
across the straw-covered ground
and move them around to expose
the squirrels' splayed backs to him.
The scattershot would hardly ever kill them,
but drop them like tops to the wooded floor.
I learned to grab them by the tail
and flail them fast against the trunk,
to listen for that hollow crack of skull on tree,
like acorns falling on a tin roof, early winter.

Fever

As a child
I caught a fever
on a weekend stay
with my father.
Having no medicine,
nor the means to get any,
he laid me down
on the plywood floor
and covered me
with every blanket
in the house, said
you must sweat
the fever out.
Days I lay there.
The fever boiled
my blood to roux.

A winter night
and my only son
is coughing.
He pulls at his ears.
I sit up with him
all night.
We rock and rock.

I dreamed my father
took me out on the boat,
night air cooling me,
water easing me to sleep.

I dreamed he drowned
me in the river.

A Lesson

I am trying to teach
my son about anger, how
it comes from me,
and mine from others,
down the line
and not his fault.
I try to teach him
how to calm himself,
the way a doe's eyes
show the fawn to lie down
without rustling. How
my father gave his anger
to me, and how, some days,
I pass it on, this inheritance.
How when Daddy said
I'll teach you a lesson,
how we'd scatter,
how the birds would flit
in the high branches, chatter
at the shadow of a man
under a wide pine ceiling.
How I was just a stalk of a boy
and lay down like marsh grass
when he was near, a sack of rice
in the shape of a boy
when he was near, and how
after a lifetime of hiding from him,
how he keeps on my mind like this,
how he is always showing up
in my poems, like this poem,
and this poem, and this poem.

The Dream of My Son

And the father tries to understand the son
who is himself a re-creation of the man
that stands before these shattered mirrors asking
Who did this, these smudges here, these crumpled
pages, this scattered mess upon the floor?
And in this dream I understand
my father's hurtful looks, when tested,
when uncontained my rage seeps out
and I am him, and my son me,
and how I must remember
the boy that stands before me now,
the times my father stayed his hand.

The Tire

And if all our thoughts are memories
then let me remember the roadside,
the high grass, the skeletal Queen Anne's Lace
you showed me when I did not know its name,
the trash along the gravel shoulder,
a single mitten, left or lost.

And just there, above the culvert in the curve,
another kind of memorial, a truck tire
nailed to a tree, full of flowers,
not wild but placed there, by loved ones
we suppose, or by the guilt-ridden maybe,
who we think might stop by on the eve
each year to remember.

And now I am remembering the four seniors killed,
graduation night, leaving a party,
not drunk, except perhaps from the buzz
of their futures between their ears.
Or the sweet freshman girl, hit
by a car just before her first football game,
and how we cheered for her that night,
and how the boys played their hearts out.

But here on the road as we ponder the tire,
the crosses nailed to trees, stuffed animals
left for a child maybe, or a mother,
I do not tell you of my own close calls,
throwing rocks at street signs
and flipping the car, four loose boys
and no seatbelts. Or the night I rode
with a boy too high to drive,

and the wheels came off the ground,
and I saw flashing before me
my own high school memorial,
a full page in the yearbook,
a boy made of flowers and crosses.

All the Men in My Family Die First

Too much sugar in my coffee,
and the half-pack of cigarettes
on the table gives less comfort these days.
Some mornings I smell the pipe
my grandfather smoked, burnt cherries,
though I can't remember his voice.
They tell me he did not speak much
after the war. My grandmother lived
twenty-five years without him.
She buried three of her four sons.
After each one smoked himself to death,
I'd sit up and visit for a while,
biscuits from scratch, and coffee,
her daily clockwork, though her laugh
lessened with each sweetened cup
until in her long silence I rose to go.

they said

they said his daddy's a sonofabitch and they said he's a drunk
and they said he ain't got no daddy noways

i try to remember everything i don't know about myself
like is he inside here somewhere just waiting to lash out of me

they said you look so much like your daddy
you so much like him i could spit

and they said he killed a man and that's why he run off
and i remember the night and the kitchen sink and maman yelling
and the blood running down his face and i know it's true

~~~

The Conversion of Saul

Once, my father
was trampled
by a horse.

The horse was blind.
Neither saw
the other coming.

There was no time
to call out,
to warn him.

After his dusty
body rolled, he rose
slightly changed.

The Dogs

Black labs, every one.
And so many that I've lost count.
Papa trained them to fetch ducks,
bounding through cold water and reeds,
across the marsh and palmetto islands.
But I remember training the pups,
in summer, warm water around our ankles
as we threw the decoys
until our shoulders ached,
and the dogs, which never tired,
would fetch and fetch themselves
to death if we let them.

And once, when Papa was away,
I shot up all of his old
beer bottles with my pellet gun,
as he taught me, not to miss.
I tossed and shot them one by one
in the water at the edge of the bank
where we trained the dogs.
And how, though Papa feared
for the dogs, it was my brother
who was cut by the glass,
when playing in the lake.

The dogs were not pets,
and Maman would not let them
in the house, and Papa
would shoot them or give them away
when they angered him
or wouldn't train.
Hundreds of them all the same.

But there was one we kept
and Papa named him Dammit,
the best dog he'd ever trained.
He had just moved us back
to the city for work,
and in the evenings
he would let the dog out
of his cage to run the streets.

I see my father now, standing
on the grass in boxer shorts,
hemmed in by houses.
Each night, as the dark settled,
he yelled across the neighborhood
over and over the name of the dog.

The Incredulity of St. Thomas

I thought he had a heart attack
but watched him crawl into bed
to sleep it off.

The next morning he slept in
and I knew then for the first time
that my father would forsake me
and die. This was his final lesson—
a body once feared could be broken.
Thirty years of labor was too short a time
to do such damage and my hands
were unburdened and guilty.
This was the gift that he left to me.

He rose after noon and tried to dress.
I put my father back to bed
and touched my finger to his ribs
to make sure he was still there.

Nocturne

On nights like these when we are tangled
and whiskey-lost, when we are enraptured,
eyes always finding each other, sunk
in a fury of our bodies' own making,
sometimes, sometimes I hear the voice
of my father, dusk-drunk and reeling,
taking me by the shoulders his face too close
to my face the smell of his breath hot and liquored,
telling me he loves me, loves the world,
loves everybody he's ever met, and everybody
he's ever hurt he didn't mean it and yes,
yes, in these moments with you I know
just what he meant, what it means
to stumble through the world and understand
just what love is.

The Deer Stand

1.

The lower door is shut. It hides
the bloated decaying hips, the atrophied
legs, the lower disproportionate half.

I see faces and faces and faces.
They come in and stare down
at my powdered face, the slack lips.

There is a darkness around
and they see it too. It is in their faces,
in their dress socks and in my suit.

No one can see my spine. If God in Heaven
set it aligned and told me to walk,
I doubt I'd remember how.

2.

I landed on my knees like a God-fearing man.
My back went limp and I crumpled, face first
in a bed of red ants.

Turning my head to the sky, I blinked
the stingers out of my eyes. I saw
the deer stand's ladder going up, up, up.

I called for you then. I couldn't
see through the burning. Knees planted
and bent like stalks in the summer heat.

3.

There is not so much to tell. I lived.
I was broken. I lived some more. I died.
From the sky to the earth and back again.

Does it make a difference that I hunted
and ate and killed, was eaten and lived?
We are ants on the face of God, scratching
and grasping, asking for more, for more.

Benediction of the Father

Midnight, father
covered in blood.
Blood from the brow,
the orbital bone,
socket, blinded.

Drunk with a broken hand.

~

From the window the marsh trembles.
Two brothers play in soil thick as black bread,
and tie-vines gather and climb unchecked
up the cinderblock stilts and swallow the house.
The eggplants in the garden are overripe,
aubergine skins fit to burst, a bruise.

~

Looking for work, hand
wrapped in duct tape.

Old classifieds cover the hole
in the tile over the sink.

The pages turn. The coffee boils down
and spackles the decanter.

Long, slow mornings.
A wasted life.

~

We lost the house.

He must have been letting things go
for a long, long time.

My father found a houseboat, said
it's time to get back to the water,
tried his hand at fishing for a living.

~

The fish slaps the pier and falls still.
Its mouth, all hook and blood,
works the air, calling.

A catfish so old and hardened
it wouldn't even suffocate.
After three shots, still,
still the fish continued to breathe.

~

The houseboat sank
the day we went back to school.
Maman wouldn't say how.
He built a house out of tin and plywood,
borrowed tools and lumber from friends.

When she left him, he burned the house.

~

He was trying to teach me something.

And what is the meaning of the broken hand,
I ask my father, who is beyond the stars and cannot answer.

I pass his words on to you.

they said

they said if you don't fight him then we'll beat your ass
so i took the three-foot branch of pine
from the side of the road and i bashed his fucking face in

i can't remember his name but i know they say it sometimes
when they're drunk and looking back and thinking about how
    good they had it
back then when we were hungry and terrible and young

they said you one of us now they said you don't never have to be
    alone now
they said you did good they said you did good they said you did
    good

ACKNOWL

EDGMENTS

Thanks to the editors of the following journals and presses where some of the poems in this collection have previously appeared, some in slightly different forms:

Bayou Magazine: "Poem with an Image of My Brother"; *Birmingham Poetry Review:* "All the Men in My Family Die First"; *Burntdistrict:* "Boy, Age 9"; *Louisiana Literature:* "Alluvial"; *The McNeese Review:* "Fever," "A Lesson," Parable," and "Remembering My Father Who Went Off to Work"; *Opossum:* "Cochon du Lait," "The Gar," and "Nocturne"; *Pembroke Magazine:* "The Incredulity of St. Thomas" and "Madonna of the Serpent"; *The Southern Review:* "Benediction of the Father," "The Conversion of Saul," "St. John the Baptist," and "they said" (all versions); *Tapestry:* "The Men on the Levee."

"Charaxos" and "Sit Still" appeared in *Odes and Elegies: Eco-Poetry from the Texas Gulf Coast* (2020); "The Dissenter's Ground" appeared in *The Dissenter's Ground* (2017); "Boy, Age 9" appeared in *Gulf Stream: Poems from the Gulf Coast* (2014); "In the Backwater," "Levee Patrol," and "The Men on the Levee" appeared in *Flood* (2013); "The Deer Stand" and "In the Backwater" appeared in *Improbable Worlds: An Anthology of Texas and Louisiana Poets* (2011).

I have a lifetime's worth of thanks to give, and inevitably I have forgotten someone. My gratitude for all of those who have helped me or urged me forward.

I want to thank my many teachers over the years, without whom this book would not have been possible. To Jack Heflin for putting me on the path. To Morri Creech for opening the gates. To Amy Fleury for being everything I need in a mentor, then and now. To Jacob Blevins for being the big brother I never had. To Marthe Reed for letting me be me. To the realest person I know, Dayana Stetco. To Ken Fields and Patrick Phillips for reminding me of home. To Louise Glück for showing me how high the mountain goes. And to Eavan Boland for changing my life.

And to the wonderful workshop leaders at festivals or residencies who I have been fortunate enough to learn from, however briefly, I thank you: Beth Ann Fennelly, Ross Gay, Marilyn Nelson, and B. H. Fairchild. Pete, thanks for the drinks.

My gratitude to all my workshop cohorts over the years, and my thanks to the following for providing time, funding, or space to write these poems: Stanford University, The University of Louisiana–Lafayette, McNeese State University, Sam Houston State University, Bread Loaf Environmental Writer's Conference, and Sewanee Writer's Conference. Thanks to Caridad Moro-Gronlier, the Plutzik Family, and The Betsy Hotel South Beach for a Writer's Room residency that allowed me to complete the final manuscript.

Endless gratitude to James W. Long and the staff of LSUP. It's been a dream. Extra special thanks to Ava Leavell Haymon, without whom this book would literally not exist.

Thanks to: David Armand, Drew Attana, Krista DeBehnke Attana, Sarah Audsley, Margaret Bashaar, Jack B. Bedell, William Brewer, Elizabeth Burk, Kai Carlson-Wee, C. S. Carrier, Grady Chambers, Elizabeth Clark, George David Clark, William Lusk Coppage, Rita D. Costello, Camille Dungy, Kevin Dwyer, Brendan Egan, Stacy Austin

Egan, Nicholas Friedman, Meg Freitag, Benjamin Garcia, Haven Gomez, J. P. Grasser, Jesse Graves, Mark Hitz, Gary Jackson, Adam Johnson, Hillary Joubert, Julie Kane, Liz Kay, Edgar Kunz, Keegan LeJeune, Esther Lin, Christopher Lowe, Katie Manning, Clare L. Martin, Erica McCreedy, Patrice Melnick, Matt W. Miller, Victoria Moore, Stella Ann Nesanovich, Dan Nowak, Leslie Jill Patterson, Alison Pelegrin, Robert Pesich, Octavio Quintanilla, Michael Rather, Jr., Gerard Robledo, Charif Shanahan, Maggie Smith, Stephanie Soileau, Essy Stone, Kevin Thomason, Jenn Alandy Trahan, Ryan Vine, William Wright, and Javier Zamora.

Beaucoup thanks to: Michael Shewmaker, Darrell Bourque, Keegan Edwards and Amanda Cappelli Edwards, the Thornhill Family, the Brasher Family, Kara Krewer and Andrew Kottwitz, Charlie Tobin and P. J. Carlisle and all the TRP crew, Jennifer Sperry Steinorth, Jessica Faust, W. Scott Thomason, and Adam Vines.

To my parents and siblings, thanks for making me who I am. I'm proud of y'all.

Nothing possible without Sarie, and nothing worth doing without Jadie and Beaux.

To Lauren Lark: If there's anything out there, I'll find you.

This book is dedicated to the ones who didn't make it out, and the ones still drowning. Lâche pas.

"The Gift at Diridon Station": Diridon Station is a Caltrain terminal in San Jose, CA.

"Remembering My Father Who Went Off to Work": A right-of-way is a strip of land that contains natural gas pipelines. Shutdowns are oil and gas refinery closures that allow for servicing and maintenance of the pipes and safety systems.

"Cochon du Lait": A community feast where a hole is dug in the ground for a pig roast. Literally "suckling pig," but full-grown feral hogs can also be used. Bagworms are the caterpillars of the bagworm moth which make pouches out of cypress needles. *Catin* has a negative connotation in France, but in Louisiana, especially in Cajun and Creole music, *catin* is used as a term of endearment, literally, "doll." *Donnez-moi mon chapeau* translates to "Catch me my hat" in Louisiana French, here meaning, "it's time to go." These lines are inspired by the song "Donnez-Moi Mon Chapeau" by Cajun accordionist Iry LeJeune.

"Float the Bones": Because of Louisiana's high water table, people in low-lying areas are often buried above ground. In flood events, water can push underground caskets to the surface.

"In the Backwater": A backwater flood is when water from a main channel backs up into its tributaries and overflows onto land. Can often occur many days or weeks after the main flood event, prolonging flooding in many areas.

"Madonna of the Serpent": *Maman* is French for mom or mama.

"The Gar": Alligator gar are prehistoric fish with rows of sharp teeth that are common in the freshwater lakes and rivers of Louisiana. *Sac-a-lait* literally means "bag of milk," and is the Louisiana French name for white perch /crappie.

"they said" (pt. 2): Angola is the largest maximum-security prison in the United States and is located in West Feliciana Parish, Louisiana. About the size of Manhattan, Angola is a former plantation surrounded by water on three sides and has no perimeter fence. Known as The Farm, it houses Louisiana's death row and execution chamber.

"The Dissenter's Ground": Poet William Blake (1757–1827) is buried in the Dissenter's burial ground at Bunhill Fields in London. The Dissenter's ground was where people who either disagreed with or left the Church of England were buried, in a section outside of the consecrated area of the cemetery. In Blake's works, the figure of Urizen, one of the Four Zoas, represents order and reason. Albion is the primeval man whose fall results in the creation of the Four Zoas. Albion is also an older name for Britain, named after a giant who was the son of Poseidon. Blake has memorials in The Poet's Corner in Westminster Abbey and St. Paul's Cathedral in London. Felpham is a village in West Sussex, England, where Blake lived for three years.

"Levee Patrol": The Great Mississippi Flood of 1927 was the largest natural disaster in American history prior to Hurricane Katrina.

The river broke its banks from Illinois to the Gulf of Mexico, and was up to eighty miles wide at some points. This flood event lasted for months and led to the creation of the modern Mississippi levee system, some of which failed again as a result of Hurricane Katrina in 2005. During the flood, levee patrols were set up to prevent attempts to dynamite the levee (which would force the water to flood the other side) and those caught on the levee risked being shot on the spot. For further reading please see *Rising Tide: The Great Mississippi Flood of 1927 and How It Changed America* by John M. Barry (Simon & Schuster, 1998).

"Charaxos": Charaxos, one of the brothers of Sappho, was a sailor. This poem is inspired by Sappho's Fragment 5.

"The Dream of My Son": Inspired by "The Dream of Lir's Son" by Eavan Boland (*New Collected Poems*, W. W. Norton, 2009)

"The Deer Stand" is for Larry Parker.

Printed in the USA
CPSIA information can be obtained
at www.ICGtesting.com
CBHW030225210524
8864CB00003B/109

9 780807 181287